Contents

1 Key features of Abacus

The Abacus programme

Abacus follows the detailed plan of teaching objectives outlined in the Framework for Teaching Mathematics. Furthermore, Abacus, from its inception, has been designed and written with precisely the same approach to the teaching of mathematics as that of the National Numeracy Strategy. Abacus is based on three principles:

Direct and interactive teaching is at the heart of the process of helping children learn mathematics. Children often do not 'discover' strategies; they have to be taught them.

Many mathematical skills and facts, particularly those which help children become fluent in mental calculations, need to be taught clearly, and then rehearsed regularly on a 'little-and-often' basis.

Materials need to support teachers in their teaching, and to help keep classroom management simple and effective. It is not necessary, nor is it desirable, for every classroom teacher to 'reinvent the wheel'. A clear structure of key objectives (with sufficient flexibility for important professional decisions to be left to each teacher in their own specific context) will minimise the hours spent planning and preparing, and maximise the teacher's effectiveness in the classroom.

As well as being based on the same philosophy, Abacus shares several assumptions with the National Numeracy Strategy.

- There will be a daily mathematics lesson.
- The lesson will have a three-part structure. Although the timing will be flexible, and will vary from lesson to lesson, class to class and school to school, the key elements will be common to all years and to all classroom contexts.
- Planning will be carried out on a weekly basis, with reference to the medium term planning grids in the Framework for Teaching Mathematics.
- In their direct teaching, with the whole class, in groups or with individuals and pairs, teachers will require simple practical resources. These will include large number lines, large number grids, medium number lines and small number grids, pupil sets of digit cards and place-value cards.

2 The National Numeracy Strategy

The National Context

The National Numeracy Strategy follows the recommendations of the final report of the Numeracy Task Force (1998) that throughout the primary phase in education there should be:

- a daily mathematics lesson of 45 to 60 minutes
- a greatly increased proportion of whole class interactive direct teaching of mathematics
- a focus on teaching mental calculation strategies.

At the heart of the National Numeracy Strategy is the Framework for Teaching Mathematics. This document provides a structured sequence of teaching objectives for each year. Put simply, it outlines the mathematical content which must be taught to each school year group. Teachers are wholly aware of the necessity for teaching a structured sequence of skills to children, particularly in relation to developing effective mental calculation strategies (we are all familiar with the problem of teaching a topic, only to find that an essential pre-requisite skill has not been covered). The Framework provides just such a programme. From September 1999, all schools in England will be expected either to draw upon the Framework for Teaching Mathematics in planning their lessons, or to ensure that their teaching programme covers a similarly complete and structured sequence of teaching objectives, with a focus on the development of mental calculation strategies.

The three-part lesson

In the National Numeracy Strategy and in Abacus, the daily mathematics lesson has the following three-part structure.

Part of lesson	What it comprises	Content includes	Abacus resources
Oral/ mental starter	Usually number work Sometimes related directly to the main teaching activity and sometimes not.	Counting (in steps of 1000, 50, 0.1, 0.5 etc.) Strategies which have already been taught Number facts (+, −, ×, ÷)	*Mental Warm-up Activities* *Simmering Activities*
Main teaching activity	One of the following: Whole class introduction to the topic, using some paired work Group work Paired investigations Individual practice	Selected objectives from an appropriate year of the Framework for Teaching Mathematics	*Teacher Cards* *Activity Books* *Workbooks* *Photocopy Masters* *Textbook*
Plenary	Validation and report on the work of children with whom you haven't worked directly Rehearsal of main teaching objective in the light of any common misconceptions Explanation of the content to be covered next	Summary of key objectives Outline of objectives to be addressed next Reinforcement activity Possible homework activity	*Teacher Cards* *Simmering Activities* *Homework Books*

There is a variety of possible formats for the middle part of the lesson, depending on:

- where in the particular topic the lesson takes place (e.g. introducing a topic, continuing or extending a topic, assessing a topic, or revising a topic)
- the nature of the mathematical topic being taught
- the age and maturity of the children
- the nature of the classroom and school (e.g. mixed-age class, small rural school, large urban school, special school or unit).

The three-part structure is flexible, and is designed to accommodate teacher's individual teaching styles as well as differences in situation, organisation and content.

It is assumed (by the National Numeracy Strategy and by Abacus) that at the start of a topic there will be more whole class teaching, whereas in the middle or towards the end of a topic, there will be more directed teaching, focused on groups, pairs or individuals. However, over the topic as a whole, there will be a substantial proportion of direct teaching of the whole class (or of the whole year group in mixed-age classes).

3 Classroom management

The Teacher Card

For each unit of work the Teacher Card identifies for you:

- the direct teaching (introductory and follow-up) to the whole class or group
- whole class activities and small group differentiated activities
- appropriate Workbook pages, Photocopy Masters and Mental Warm-up Activities
- ideas for Plenaries.

This enables you to plan effectively for the whole class (large or small), covering a wide range of ability.

Children will experience a range of tasks within each unit, the actual composition determined by you following the guidance on the Teacher Card.

Classroom organisation

Abacus allows for flexibility in the organisation of the children. On the assumption that the teaching takes place with the whole class, this can be followed using a variety of different organisational structures. Examples include:

- the whole class working together on the same activity, possibly in pairs
- half of the class working on one Activity, whilst the other half work on another Activity
- a 'carousel' of Activities, with the children in groups, moving from one activity to another
- half of the children working in groups on Activities, whilst the other half are working on material in the Workbooks, Textbook or Photocopy Masters.

Organising groups

- You will decide on the best organisation of groups to suit your needs at any time. There should be no more than three levels of work in a single-age class, and no more than four levels in a mixed-age class.
- The composition of the groups will vary depending on the unit of work being studied.
- You can plan within your group structure, how, during the unit, you can work in a focused way with any one group.
- You will need to judge how much time to allow for different children to complete any task. The carousel nature of the tasks provides versatility in management.
- Other adults can be used to assist with the activities.
- Some children in the class may be used occasionally in a peer-tutoring role within the activity carousel.

4 The Abacus materials

Mental Warm-up Activities

The Mental Warm-up Activities Book provides a comprehensive scheme of work for developing mental mathematics strategies. Each day you will select an appropriate activity to take place before the main part of the lesson. The activities are designed to rehearse and sharpen key mental mathematics skill, including counting, comparing and ordering numbers. They allow you to get off to a clear, crisp start to the lesson.

Each unit includes a 'word of the week', 'shape of the week' or 'number of the week' which helps the children to extend their vocabulary and to begin to generate statements about familiar mathematical concepts.

N2 Place-value

Show me

Two less

Number cards (0 to 9), one set per pair

Ask the children to show you the number card that is two less than 3; then 9; then 6; then 2; then 8; then 4; then 11; then 10; then 5. For example, when you say *three*, they show you the 1 card.

Stick there

Tens and units

Two dice and cubes

Put the children into two teams. Write *T* and *U* on the board for each team. The children take turns to throw the dice for their team.
They write the number they have thrown on the board in either the tens or the units column for their team, trying to make the largest number possible.
When each team has written two digits on the board, they all read the 2-digit number they have created.
Compare numbers. Which is the larger? That team gets a cube.
Play until one team has seven cubes.

Shape of the week — cube

Sample tasks
- it is a solid (3-d) shape
- some bricks and some boxes are cube shaped
- it has 6 faces which are all squares
- it has 8 corners
- it has 12 edges
- two cubes joined together make a cuboid

2

N3 Addition

Story maths

Coin recognition

Several 1p, 2p and 5p coins

Tell the children a brief story. *One day, Ilesh was out walking on the beach near his home. He was walking along the edge of the water when something glistening in the sand beneath the waves caught his eye. It was two coins! Very excited, Ilesh picked the coins up. He realised that they added up to 10p in all. Which two coins had he found?* Give the children 2 or 3 minutes' thinking time and then take suggestions. Use real coins to demonstrate the answer. Tell a similar story with different coins.

Number lines

Addition pairs to 10

Write on the board *This and what makes 10?*
Then write these numbers in a column on the left-hand side of the board: 5, 4, 7, 10, 8, 3, 6, 9, 2, 0, 1.
Go down the list and choose different children to write alongside each the number that, when added to it, makes 10.

This and what makes 10?
5
4
7
10

Number of the week — 10

Sample tasks
- Count in twos to our number, and beyond.
- Count in tens from our number. Repeat for fives.
- Say two numbers which add to our number. e.g. 1 and 9.
- Add our number to 3, 17, 24, ...
- Take our number from 17, 11, 23, ...

Sample facts
- pairs which make 10 are 0 and 10, 1 and 9, 2 and 8, ...
- it is the first 2-digit number
- it is in the 'twos', the 'tens' and the 'fives'
- it is the number of 1p coins in 10p, the number of 10p coins in £1
- it is the number of 10 cm strips in 1 metre
- it is the number of toes we each have

3

Teacher Cards

The main teaching for the lesson is supported by the Teacher Cards. The front of each Teacher Card provides:

- support for the whole class teaching on the first day of a topic
- a list of the key teaching points addressed by the Unit
- a list of any materials necessary for the teaching
- key vocabulary either introduced or used during the course of the Unit.

N2 Place-value

Teaching points
- To read and write numbers to at least 100
- To recognise the relationship between tens and units
- To estimate a number of objects up to 50
- To order 2-digit numbers

Materials
- Medium number cards (1 to 100)
- Coins (nine 1p and 10p)
- Interlocking cubes (nine towers of ten, and some loose cubes)

Key words
- tens
- units/ones
- smallest

Teaching
- Give ten children a number card (between 20 and 100). *Look carefully at your number. What does it begin with?*
- Start writing the numbers from 20 to 100 on the board. Ask the children to count in unison as you do this. When you reach the first number held by one of the children e.g. 23, they should call out. Stop and ask him to come and show the class. *Which number is this?*
- Show the children the coins. *What coins do we need to make Jo's number?* Help him to take two 10p coins and three 1p coins. *Twenty-three has two tens.* Point to the '2' in 23. *Twenty-three has three ones (or three units).* Point to the '3' in 23.
- Choose another child. *What cubes should she take to make twenty-three?* Help her to take two towers of ten cubes and three loose cubes. *Twenty-three has two tens.* Take two towers of ten cubes. *Twenty-three has three ones (or three units).* Take three loose cubes. Point to the separate parts of the number on the board again.
- Continue writing the numbers in order on the board until the next number held by one of the children is called out, e.g. 34. *Come and show the class. Which number is this?* Ask the class *Which coins should she take?* Help her to take three 10p coins and four 1p coins. Choose another child to take that number of cubes. *What cubes should he take?* Help him to take three towers of ten cubes and four loose cubes. *Thirty-four has three tens and four ones (or four units).*
- Continue counting and writing the numbers on the board. Each time you reach a number held by one of the children, ask them to call out and show it to the class. Use either the coins or the cubes to demonstrate the amount.

2 N2

4. The Abacus materials

The back of each Teacher Card provides:

- support for further teaching for a subsequent day
- references to differentiated practical activities, including materials and learning outcomes (which are presented in a separate Activity Book)
- guidance on key points, common misconceptions etc., for use during plenary sessions
- references to additional Abacus resources: Mental Warm-up Activities, Workbooks, Textbook, Photocopy Masters.

N2 Place-value

Materials

- Number cards (10 to 99), Base Ten material (tens and units)

Teaching

- Give a random number card to ten children. Choose one of the children to hold up his card, e.g. 34. Choose another child to collect a matching amount of Base Ten material. Ask the class *How many tens? Three. How many units? Four. Three tens and four units. Thirty-four.*
- Repeat for each child. When the tenth child is standing at the front, ask the class *Which number is the smallest?* E.g. 17. *Stand here (facing the class), on the left. What is the next smallest number?* E.g. 24. *Stand next to seventeen.* Continue like this, until all ten numbers are in order.
- Choose different children in the row. *How many tens?* E.g. 6. *How many units?* E.g. 9. *Sixty-nine, six tens and nine units.*
- Repeat for a different set of ten children.

2 Warm-up Activities | 2 Activity Book | 4–6 Number Workbook 1 | 3 Photocopy Masters

ACTIVITY 1 — *Whole class, in groups of 3*

Number cards (1 to 100) (PCMs 2 to 8), interlocking cubes, coins (10p, 1p)
Recognising the number of tens and units in a 2-digit number

ACTIVITY 2 — *4 children*

Number cards (1 to 100) (PCMs 2 to 8), calculator, interlocking cubes, coins (10p, 1p)
Recognising the number of tens and units in a 2-digit number

ACTIVITY 3 — *4 children*

Place-value cards (tens and units) (PCMs 10 to 12), counters
Recognising tens and units in a 2-digit number, ordering 2-digit numbers

ACTIVITY 4 — *3-4 children*

Number grid 2 (PCM 14), grid window (PCM 17), coins (10p, 1p)
Recognising the number of tens and units in a 2-digit number

ACTIVITY 5 — *2-4 children*

Infant game 13: 'Number Crunch', coin, counters
Recognising and reading numbers (up to 100)

Plenaries

Key points

- Recognising that the '2' and '3' in the number '23' are called digits. 23 is a 2-digit number.
- Recognising that in a 2-digit number, the first digit shows how many tens, the second digit shows how many ones (or units).
- Knowing that the smallest 2-digit number is 10, the largest is 99.

Common difficulty

- Not understanding the concept of tens and units. (Help by providing plenty of activities matching 2-digit numbers with: (a) Base Ten material (b) towers of cubes and loose cubes, (c) 10p and 1p coins, (d) place-value cards.

Activity

You say a number of tens and units. E.g. *Three tens and six units.* The children have to say the 2-digit number, i.e. *Thirty-six.* Repeat for different numbers.

The Teacher Cards are divided into two sets: *Number* and *Shape, Space and Measures*. A suggested teaching order, and how this fits with the National Numeracy Framework Planning Grids are given at the end of this book. There are other possible routes through the materials, and the *Shape, Space and Measures* units are presented in a separate block to allow you easily to re-order them.

Activity Book

N2 **Place-value**

ACTIVITY 1 Whole class, in groups of 3 children

- *Recognising the number of tens and units in a 2-digit number*

Number cards (1 to 100) (PCMs 2 to 8) one set per group, interlocking cubes (loose and in towers of ten)/coins (1p, 10p)

The children shuffle the cards and place them face down in a pile. They take turns to reveal a card. Together they must match the card with the correct number of either cubes or coins. Choose groups to show their number and matching set of cubes or coins. Repeat.

ACTIVITY 2 4 children

- *Recognising the number of tens and units in a 2-digit number*

Number cards (1 to 100) (PCMs 2 to 8), a calculator, interlocking cubes (loose and in towers of ten), coins (1p, 10p)

The first child enters a 2-digit number on the calculator and shows it to the second and third child but not to the fourth child. The second child matches the number with 10p and 1p coins. The third child matches the number with interlocking cubes. The fourth child looks at the cubes and the coins and selects the matching number card. They check on the calculator. Does the card match? Repeat the activity, swapping roles.

ACTIVITY 3 4 children

- *Recognising the number of tens and units in a 2-digit number*
- *Ordering 2-digit numbers*

Place-value cards (tens and units) (PCMs 10 to 12), counters

Shuffle the cards and place them face down in two piles. Each child takes one tens and one units card and creates a 2-digit number. They take turns to say their number, and how many tens and units there are in the number. Ask the children to place the numbers in order. The children with the smallest and largest numbers take a counter each. Let them replace the cards and play again several times. Who collects the most counters?

ACTIVITY 4 3-4 children

- *Recognising the number of tens and units in a 2-digit number*

Number grid 2 (PCM 14), grid window (PCM 17), coins (1p, 10p)

One child places the window on the grid to outline a 2-digit number, e.g. 5 and 8 showing 58. He hides it from the other children and matches the number with coins, i.e. five 10p and eight 1p coins. He removes the window and then shows the coins to the other children. The other children take the grid and have to outline the same 2-digit number. Repeat, taking turns to outline numbers.

ACTIVITY 5 2-4 children

- *Recognising and reading numbers (up to 100)*

Infant game 13: 'Number Crunch', a coin, a counter each

(See instructions on the card.)

2

The Activity Book includes all the practical activities which will follow the introductory teaching. Each Unit of the programme is supported by a range of activities, covering different styles, learning objectives, numbers of children and resources, which are fully referenced on each Teacher Card. Most units include an Activity which may be taught to the whole class. Such activities are indicated by the icon:

Each activity includes the following information:

- appropriate number of children
- a list of relevant materials and 'specialist' resources (provided as Photcopy Masters at the back of the book)
- level of difficulty, indicated by a simple code: basic work, for all children, enrichment and extension
- learning points are also provided. These will assist the teacher in directing the group and in making informal assessments.

Workbooks

There are four Workbooks in Abacus 2, three for *Number* and one for *Shape, Space and Measures*. Each Workbook page offers consolidation of the practical work covered by you and gives evidence of the children's progress through the scheme.

On each page, the relevant Abacus Unit is identified, along with a heading, which highlights the mathematical content of the page and reinforces key vocabulary. A key feature of the pages is the inclusion of 'Extras' (coded), which provide additional activities usually with an investigational or practical focus away from the Workbook page. Relevant Workbook pages are referenced on each Teacher Card.

Photocopy Masters

The Photocopy Masters contain activities to enhance the children's learning and are identified on the relevant Teacher Cards. They include:

- more work for reinforcement
- extension and enrichment material
- games, and other shared, practical activities.

The Photocopy Masters are coded in the same way as the practical activities: ● basic work, ●● for all children, ●●● enrichment and extension.

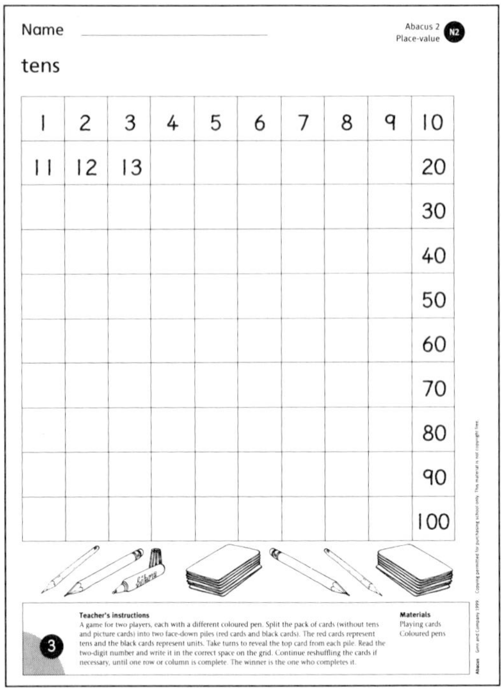
Name

Abacus 2 N2
Place-value

tens

1	2	3	4	5	6	7	8	9	10
11	12	13							20
									30
									40
									50
									60
									70
									80
									90
									100

3

Teacher's instructions
A game for two players, each with a different coloured pen. Split the pack of cards (without tens and picture cards) into two face-down piles (red cards and black cards). The red cards represent tens and the black cards represent units. Take turns to reveal the top card from each pile. Read the two-digit number and write it in the correct space on the grid. Continue reshuffling the cards if necessary, until one row or column is complete. The winner is the one who completes it.

Materials
Playing cards
Coloured pens

Abacus Ginn and Company 1999. Copying permitted for purchasing school only. This material is not copyright free.

Resource Bank and Infant Games

The Resource Bank provides the essential materials needed for the teaching and practical activities in the programme. The basic resources you need for Year Two are recommended on page 34, but the Resource Bank gives you the flexibility to order additional sets of materials to suit your particular needs. Items include: group and class sets of number cards, place-value cards, wall charts and number line cards.

The Infant Games pack provides 24 games aimed at practising skills relating to specific Teacher Card units. They are included as activities in the Activity Book.

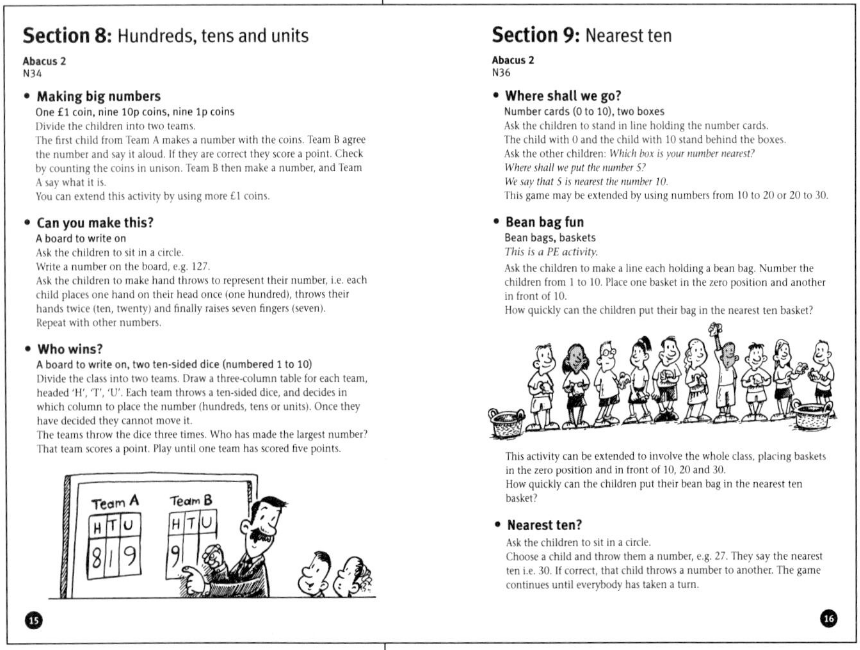
Section 8: Hundreds, tens and units

Abacus 2
N34

- **Making big numbers**
  One £1 coin, nine 10p coins, nine 1p coins
  Divide the children into two teams.
  The first child from Team A makes a number with the coins. Team B agree the number and say it aloud. If they are correct they score a point. Check by counting the coins in unison. Team B then make a number, and Team A say what it is.
  You can extend this activity by using more £1 coins.
- **Can you make this?**
  A board to write on
  Ask the children to sit in a circle.
  Write a number on the board, e.g. 127.
  Ask the children to make hand throws to represent their number, i.e. each child places one hand on their head once (one hundred), throws their hands twice (ten, twenty) and finally raises seven fingers (seven).
  Repeat with other numbers.
- **Who wins?**
  A board to write on, two ten-sided dice (numbered 1 to 10)
  Divide the class into two teams. Draw a three-column table for each team, headed 'H', 'T', 'U'. Each team throws a ten-sided dice, and decides in which column to place the number (hundreds, tens or units). Once they have decided they cannot move it.
  The teams throw the dice three times. Who has made the largest number? That team scores a point. Play until one team has scored five points.

Team A
H T U
8 1 9
Team B
H T U
9

15

Section 9: Nearest ten

Abacus 2
N36

- **Where shall we go?**
  Number cards (0 to 10), two boxes
  Ask the children to stand in line holding the number cards.
  The child with 0 and the child with 10 stand behind the boxes.
  Ask the other children: *Which box is your number nearest?*
  Where shall we put the number 5?
  We say that 5 is nearest the number 10.
  This game may be extended by using numbers from 10 to 20 or 20 to 30.
- **Bean bag fun**
  Bean bags, baskets
  This is a PE activity.
  Ask the children to make a line each holding a bean bag. Number the children from 1 to 10. Place one basket in the zero position and another in front of 10.
  How quickly can the children put their bag in the nearest ten basket?
  This activity can be extended to involve the whole class, placing baskets in the zero position and in front of 10, 20 and 30.
  How quickly can the children put their bean bag in the nearest ten basket?
- **Nearest ten?**
  Ask the children to sit in a circle.
  Choose a child and throw them a number, e.g. 27. They say the nearest ten i.e. 30. If correct, that child throws a number to another. The game continues until everybody has taken a turn.

16

Simmering Activities

Relevant rhymes, quick-recalls, games and other activities are contained in the Simmering Activities book. The activities require little or no preparation and are brief enough to be carried out in just a few minutes – at registration or in the dinner queue. Once introduced, the activity can be used regularly to allow the concept or skill to keep 'simmering'.

Homework Book

The Homework Book provides a valuable opportunity for shared activities between the parent and child. A range of activities are included (shared mathematics tasks, games, memorisation activities, investigative or problem-solving activities), one for each Unit of the programme. Some activities are more formal practice, whilst others are more informal shared activities.

50 beans

Numbers to 100 N1

A person to play with, and small objects such as dried beans, peas, pasta shapes or small Lego bricks

Each guess what 50 beans looks like, and try to take that many each without counting.

Now each count your beans by grouping them in 5s.

Write down how many you took. Who was closest?

Together count exactly 50, put them in a small bag and bring them into school.

Making 12 numbers

Place-value N2

10 40 80

5 1 7 6

Look at these cards. Using 2 cards, make a 2-digit number.

40 5 → 45

How many different numbers can you make? Write them down. (There are 12 altogether.)

Which is the largest? Which is the smallest?

In class Use real place value cards or let some children take cards home to help them.

1

Assessment Book

The Assessment Book provides photocopiable assessment sheets, and teacher guidance for each unit of the programme. The teacher's notes include a summary of the skills assessed, diagnostic advice, activities for children who require further consolidation and oral, mental maths questions.

N1 Numbers to 100 N2 Place-value

Numbers to 100

Skills summary

- To say the number names, in sequence, from zero to 100
- To say the number names, in sequence, from 100 to zero
- To count a set of objects up to 100
- To match a spoken number name to its written numeral (up to 100)
- To match a written numeral to its spoken number name (up to 100)
- To estimate a number of objects up to 50
- To recognise the relationship between tens and units

Diagnostic materials

Number Workbook 1, page 1
- Check children can write the numbers to 30, in order.

Number Workbook 1, page 4
- Check children recognise the tens and units in a 2-digit number.

Oral questions

Read each question twice. Allow about ten seconds after each reading.

1. Write 21.
2. Write the next number: 28, 29, 30, ...
3. How many tens in this number (write '45' on the board)?
4. How many cubes? (Hold up three sticks of 10 and four loose cubes.)

Common difficulties

When counting, check that the children are able to bridge into new tens confidently. Check that they are saying the number names correctly – provide plenty of practice (counting in unison, or as individuals around the class).
When reading and writing numbers, emphasise the patterns involved (some children may reverse the digits, e.g. writing 37 for 73). The number grid provides a useful visual aid for highlighting the patterns involved.
Discourage children from trying to give a precise answer when estimating (e.g. 32). Ask questions like: *Is it nearer 30 or 40?*

Practice activities

1. Take one or two handfuls of cubes and quickly estimate how many. Count the cubes to check (make sure you count them accurately – try grouping in twos).
2. Take a handful of 10p coins (up to ten) and a handful of 1p coins (up to 10). Estimate how much, then check by counting.

Answers

1. 21	**2.** 31	**3.** 4	**4.** 14
5. 13	**6.** 39, 41	**7.** 30, 31	**8.** 88, 90
9. 6	**10.** 8	**11.** 32p	**12.** 55p

6

Name ______________ N1 N2

1. ☐ 2. ☐ 3. ☐ 4. ☐   /4

Write the missing numbers.

5. 12 ☐ 14   6. ☐ 40 ☐

7. 29 ☐ ☐   8. ☐ 89 ☐   /4

Write how many tens.

9. 63 → ☐ tens   10. 81 → ☐ tens   /2

Write the totals.

11.  ☐ p

12. 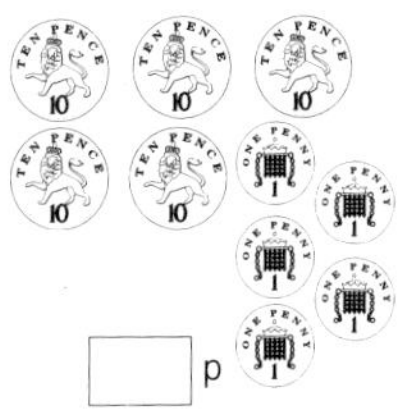 ☐ p   /2

Score: ☐/12   Total: ☐

Challenge Book

The Challenge Book is aimed at pupils requiring further enrichment and reinforcement within a Unit. The Challenge Book provides a photocopiable sheet, and teacher's notes for each Unit, so that more able children will either:

- extend their mathematical understanding beyond the focus of the Unit
- broaden their understanding of the particular topic they are studying.

The challenges require minimal teacher input and use of additional materials.

Name

N1 N2

Card numbers

Use these four cards.

2 5 9 7

Make as many different 2-digit numbers as you can from these four cards.

Here are some:

25 57

There are 12 altogether.

Write them in order, from smallest to largest.

ABACUS 2 CHALLENGE MASTER 1

Number Textbook

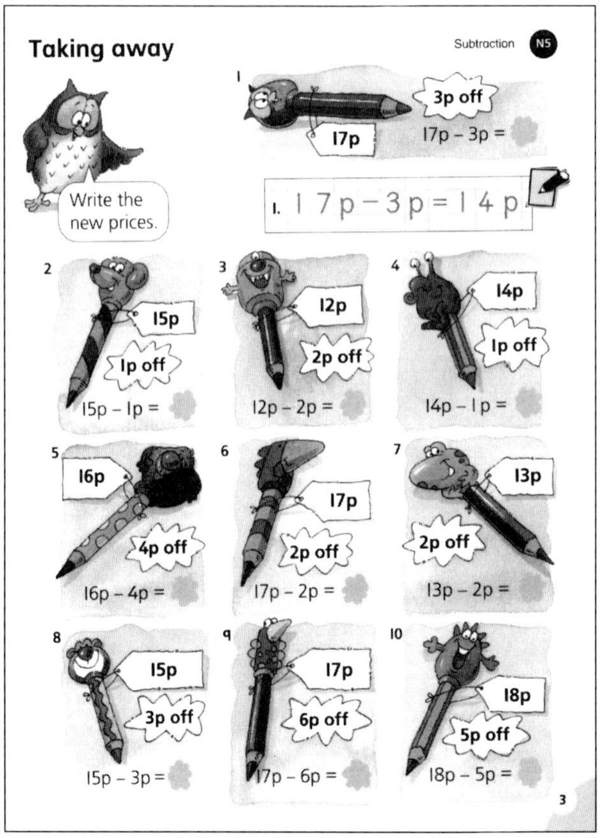
Taking away

Subtraction N5

Write the new prices.

1. 17p 3p off 17p − 3p =

1. 17p − 3p = 14p

2. 15p 1p off 15p − 1p =

3. 12p 2p off 12p − 2p =

4. 14p 1p off 14p − 1p =

5. 16p 4p off 16p − 4p =

6. 17p 2p off 17p − 2p =

7. 13p 2p off 13p − 2p =

8. 15p 3p off 15p − 3p =

9. 17p 6p off 17p − 6p =

10. 18p 5p off 18p − 5p =

3

The Number Textbook provides valuable opportunities for all children to start to interpret instructions and take responsibility for recording and organising their own work. The Textbook provides pages of consolidation and extension for many of the Number Units, and is accessible to most pupils.

5 An Abacus Unit

Abacus was conceived with the identical approach to teaching as the National Numeracy Strategy. The New Abacus unit matches precisely the structure of a sequence of linked three-part lessons through a topic. As an illustration, the planning for a typical Year 2 lesson (adding 2-digit numbers mentally) is shown below.

	Day 1	**Day 2**	**Day 3**
Mental/oral starter	Practise a necessary pre-requisite skill, e.g. counting in tens	Rehearse number bonds to ten to help with quick arithmetic	Play a 'bingo' game, adding 11 and 12 to 2-digit numbers
Main teaching activity	1. Introduce topic to whole class, using a large number grid (1 to 100) as a model and demonstrating how to add multiples of ten and then add units, e.g. 34 + 23 = 34 + 20 + 3. 2. Children all do brief practice activity in workbooks, teacher working with least able group.	1. Briefly rehearse the main teaching point, using the number grid. 2. Children work in 4 groups. Teacher works with less able children, providing a hands-on activity and further teaching. 'Middle' two groups work independently on written practice. More able children work on an extension activity.	1. Rehearse the main teaching point, using a different model (e.g. 10p and 1p coins, place-value cards). 2. Children work in pairs and individually on a graded task using money and/or place-value cards as appropriate, and recording their work in their mathematics book. 3. Assess children's work, looking at how far they progressed with graded task
Plenary	Rehearse the main point and play a game to practise the method.	Feedback from middle two groups and more able to whole class. Address some common difficulties.	Rehearse main teaching point through common difficulty. Summarise what the children have learned.

5. An Abacus Unit

Immediately it is clear that the Abacus materials have been designed to fit the structure shown in the above topic plan.

	Day 1	**Day 2**	**Day 3**
Mental/oral starter	Mental Warm-up Activities *(Practise a necessary pre-requisite skill)*	Mental Warm-up Activities *(Rehearse number bonds)*	Mental Warm-up Activities *(Play a 'bingo' game)*
Main teaching activity	1. Teacher card front *(Introduce topic to whole class)* 2. Activity Book and number grids *(Brief practice activity)*	1. Teacher card front and first activity (whole class) *(Rehearse the main teaching point)* 2. Activities from the Activity Book, Workbooks, Photocopy Masters or Textbook *(Children work in four groups)*	1. Teacher card back *(Rehearse the main teaching point, using different model)* 2. Workbook and/or Activity book *(Children work in pairs and individually on a graded task)* 3. Assessment book *(Assess children's work)*
Plenary	Teacher card back *(Rehearse the main point and play a game)*	Teacher card back *(Address some common difficulties)*	Teacher card back *(Rehearse main teaching point through common difficulty)*

Supporting teachers in teaching and children in learning

Abacus is founded on the idea that teachers need to be in control of how and when they teach a particular piece of mathematics to their class. It is the teacher, and not the materials, which make the professional decisions. Therefore the Abacus materials have been designed to allow you to decide:

- how long to spend on any one topic
- how to structure that topic – the proportion of time spent on whole class teaching, group work, individual or paired practice, assessment and revision
- how to time the different parts of the lesson – the length of mental/oral sections, direct teaching, practice
- the order in which to teach the topics
- how to relate the teaching of number and non-number topics.

Flexibility in the teaching of each topic

Whilst the Abacus planning grids (from page 42) have been designed to match the medium term planning grids in the Numeracy Framework, a degree of flexibility is nevertheless built in. Abacus allows you to structure each topic as you see fit. Some topics may be completed in two days, and some will run over three days, and it is up to you how long to remain on any one topic. In Abacus, as in the Framework, there is often a sequence of related topics, and the practice of some of the key skills may therefore continue over two, or even three, topics. This allows for the maximum reinforcement of the basic skills and facts.

Flexibility in classroom management

The basic Abacus model enables you to decide how best to structure the main teaching activity. Each Teacher Card is structured to provide a minimum of two whole class teaching sessions, drawing upon different models or images in demonstrating the topic to the children. The Activity Book supplies a variety of activities, from those for use with the whole class to those directed at small groups or pairs. The Workbooks and Photocopy Masters allow for structured and appropriate levels of practice, and again these can be used individually or in pairs, or to structure some group work. The activities in the Assessment Book enable teachers to structure their own assessment and evaluation tasks, and to practise the skills needed for the Standard Tasks and Tests at the end of each Key Stage.

Teaching in mixed-age classes

The order of the Abacus Teacher Cards matches closely the order of topics outlined in the medium term planning grids in the Numeracy Framework. This means that there is a planned overlap in the order of topics for years 1, 2 and 3, and also for years 4, 5 and 6. It is therefore quite possible to plan and teach a topic to two or more year groups, moving across from one set of objectives to another.

With Abacus, the organisation of this becomes quite simple. You select the appropriate Teacher Cards from each year, e.g. Years 1 and 2. The pre-requisite skills for these cards will then allow you to select a mental/oral activity which can be carried out with the whole class (from the Mental Warm-up Activities for Years 1 or 2). You can then move on to some direct teaching, following the selected Year 1 Teacher Card. (The Year 2 children can either participate as a recap, or work independently on a prepared activity.) Later, or on the second day, it will be possible to move on to some direct teaching with Year 2, from the appropriate Teacher Card, whilst Year 1 children are engaged in relevant follow-up work.

Starting the lesson

As we know, the way a lesson starts can often dictate the direction of subsequent teaching. If a lesson gets off to a crisp, clear start, the children are likely to be well prepared to engage with the main topic being taught. The National Numeracy Strategy suggests that the first ten minutes of the lesson should be allocated to the practice and reinforcement of those skills and facts which benefit from a 'little and often' approach. In this category are included:

- counting in steps of different sizes, both forwards and backwards
- instant recall of number facts, including discussing ways of remembering the facts that need to be learned by heart
- previously-taught mental strategies.

It is not appropriate to introduce topics for the first time in this mental/oral part of the lesson, and neither should complex operations be explained. It is a time for 'quick-fire' rehearsal of basic skills, for using a strategy that has already been taught, or for choosing an operation to solve a problem quickly.

This part of the session will almost always be number work, although occasionally it may focus on a particular aspect of shape or of measures, such as 'time'. Importantly, it is not necessarily related to the second part of the lesson. For example, a teacher planning a lesson on 2-d shape could (and often would) include a starter activity on number.

This part of the lesson involves working with the whole class and only exceptionally would it be necessary to work with a group or to exempt individuals from the session. The Abacus Mental Warm-up Activities have been specifically written to address this part of the lesson, and provide a wide variety of whole class oral and mental activities for each day's teaching.

Main teaching activity

The function of the main part of the lesson can vary, depending upon various factors (where you are in a topic, the age and maturity of the children etc.). It can provide time for:

- introducing a new topic
- extending previous work and developing children's understanding
- practising a skill or strategy
- using and applying what has been learned
- assessing children's learning
- revising or revisiting a topic.

During the main teaching activity, the teacher can choose how to organise the class. It is quite possible that the lesson you teach on a Monday will have quite a different style of classroom organisation from the lesson you teach on Tuesday. Clearly, the way you choose to organise the class will be guided by the purpose of the lesson (is it introducing a new topic, or rehearsing an old one?). It will also dictate, to some extent, the teaching strategy you use. For example, a whole class lesson could require a higher percentage of demonstration or explanation, whilst a lesson where groups of children are working together could involve more discussion or description. Taking all these factors into account, on any one day a teacher can choose to organise the class:

- as a whole class session, with direct teaching of the whole class or with a paired investigation
- with the children working in groups, and the teacher working in a focused way with one or two of the groups
- with the children working on a task in pairs or as individuals.

Although the Numeracy Strategy explicitly encourages a flexible approach to the organisation of the main teaching activity, it is clear about three central points:

- the need for teachers to organise the class to fit the purpose of the lesson
- that, although any one lesson may not involve a high proportion of direct teaching of the whole class (or year group) nevertheless, over the complete unit, more than 50% of the teaching is likely to be of this form
- that emphasis should be placed on keeping the children together, so it would not be appropriate to set more than three levels of work for any one year group, and no more than two levels of work per year group in a mixed-age range class (though, clearly, specific provision must be made for particular children who have individual education plans).

It is clear (both from the final report of the Numeracy Task Force, and the National Numeracy Strategy itself) that at the heart of the teaching and learning process is the active, direct teaching of a topic. In order to focus on this, teachers need to have:

- a clear objective for each lesson and a set of objectives for the topic
- a definite 'way of teaching' – an image or model (e.g. number line, money) which will be used to represent or demonstrate the mathematics
- a variety of teaching strategies to ensure that the lesson is interactive.

The Abacus Teacher Cards have been designed with these three requirements in mind.

- They provide a clear set of objectives for each unit, with specific learning objectives for each activity.
- They outline the model to be used in teaching the mathematics, and make clear the careful use of vocabulary.
- They also provide a variety of teaching strategies, through the work with the whole class, the group activities, the individual and paired practice and the extra support provided by the Simmering Activities and the Infant Games.

The plenary session

Plenary sessions can often be the hardest part of the lesson to teach successfully. The children (and the teacher!) are tired, and some will require more feedback than others, meaning that boredom may cause disruption. It is hard to plan the plenary session because it will often develop from what has occurred during the lesson.

The purpose of the plenary as explained by the Numeracy Strategy is threefold. It allows time for:

- A rehearsal of the main teaching points and summary of the key facts. This is the vital, 'What have we learned today?' part of the lesson.
- Children to present their work to you and others, particularly those who may have been working independently during the main part of the lesson.
- Addressing any difficulties that may have arisen during the lesson.
- Forward planning – helping to make explicit what we are going to do next, and perhaps outlining any homework.

Rehearsing the main teaching points of the lesson is very important for two reasons. Firstly, it allows you to ensure that the learning objectives have been clearly articulated and that children have taken this in. Secondly, it enables you to pick up any difficulties that several children may have shared. Frequently there will be common misconceptions or errors which it can prove useful to address with the whole class. This is not to point out children who have made mistakes, but rather to use common errors as a way of rehearsing the teaching points.

The Abacus Teacher Cards highlight the key learning points and also provide advice on probable common misconceptions which may occur when teaching that particular topic. This will allow you to plan how to address such misconceptions, as well as preparing you to look out for difficulties which are encountered by several children.

Taking feedback from children is difficult to do in a way which does not leave some of the class feeling bored or frustrated. It helps to vary the format of their presentation. For example:

- ask some children to write the hardest or easiest question they had to do on the board
- give some children a poster or a strip of paper to record some or all of their work during an activity, so that they can display this
- ask a group to show their work and then choose a question to ask the rest of the class
- choose a pair of children to demonstrate a strategy they have been using
- choose some children to write the answer to a question on the board. The rest of the class have to guess what the question was.

The plenary can also be made easier by discussing a group of children's work with them, and then marking it together just before you bring the whole class together. That group can then show the children their work by showing any pieces you felt were particularly special.

The plenary should end with a suggestion about where the children are going next in mathematics. You may be going to extend the work you did today, or start a new topic. Sometimes you will want to give the class a formal homework task, and on other occasions it will be a more informal activity (e.g. *look out for car numbers that end in '5'. Can you remember one to tell me tomorrow?*).

The plenary should be kept short – a protracted ending will not improve the lesson or make the children learn any more. The lesson needs to be brought to a sharp close, and the plenary enables the teacher to evaluate its success.

Homework

It is important to bear in mind the purposes of homework. A reasonable list might include:

- To involve the parents in their children's learning.
- To help parents keep abreast of what their child can and cannot do.
- To utilise the context of the home and apply some numerical strategies in a non-school situation.
- To encourage parents and children to talk about their number work and for children to explain what they are doing and how.
- To extend the time for learning mathematics and give some extra practice in number work.
- to help parents improve, extend or practise their own numerical strategies.

It is a well-established fact that simply sending home extra mathematics will have little or no effect on many children's attainment, unless effort is made to involve and include their parents in their learning. Therefore, in planning and setting homework, it is important that schools consider the following.

How much and how often?

Little and fairly frequently is better than lots occasionally. It is good to have specific and regular homework 'nights' so that parents and children grow to expect it. An ideal schedule is a shared task at the weekend, so that parents can get involved, and more traditional individual homework once or twice a week, depending on the age of the child.

What type?

Homework is most effective when it is varied – some types of homework might include:

- Shared mathematics tasks, games or other activities where the child discusses the mathematics. The task itself might draw upon the home context.
- Memorisation games or activities to help children with the instant recall of number facts.
- Tasks or activities which help children practise number strategies or skills introduced in school.
- Investigative or problem-solving activities where the child, and the parent, explore an aspect of mathematics together.

The Abacus Homework Books have been planned to include a range of these types of activity. How many parents get involved with the shared activities is not only dependent on the catchment area of the school – research indicates that the attitude of the teachers and the school is a very important factor. By holding meetings, talking to parents, feeding back information and trying to keep them involved, the school can make a huge difference to the number of parents who play an active role in their child's education.

Who is it for?

All children can be encouraged to share mathematics activities with their parents (though the proportion of homework to be done independently will increase as children get older). However, no child should be excluded from an activity because they have difficulty finding a partner to share the task at home. Wherever possible provision for repeating or extending the shared task in the context of school (or at an after school club) should be made.

Assessment

Opportunities for informal assessment occur throughout many of the aspects of an Abacus unit.

The Mental Warm-up Activities offer opportunities for observational assessment, both for the whole class and for individuals. The continuous feedback in the form of child response to these tasks provides immediate observational measures of performance. The opportunities in this stage of the unit for you to set tasks for varying levels of ability inform further when assessing the feedback.

Similarly, during the Plenary sessions, observational assessment opportunities are numerous.

Additional opportunities are provided during the main teaching, both during the interactive element of the teaching, and particularly when the children are engaged in group activities, and you are focusing on a chosen group.

Assessment of the childrens' written work is provided from completed Workbook and Textbook pages and Photocopy Masters and can be recorded using the Assessment grids on page 36 and 37.

The Assessment Book offers comprehensive support material for assessing children's progress, within each unit or small set of units. This range includes: a written assessment sheet, oral assessment questions, and suggested sections of the Workbook to use for diagnostic purposes. Also included are common diffficulties, and suggested practical activities to help overcome these.

6 Differentiation

The National Numeracy Strategy emphasises the need to keep the children together. This links to the requirement that, over a period of time, the proportion of whole class direct teaching should be more than 50% (indeed, it is easy to see how this figure could be closer to 75% in a single year group, given that the mental starter and plenary both involve working with the whole class).

Whole class focus

Although any one lesson may not involve a high proportion of whole class direct teaching, over a complete topic, more than 50% of the teaching is likely to be with the whole class.

Keeping the children together

Emphasis should be placed on keeping the children together, so that it would not be appropriate to set more than three levels of work for any one year group, and no more than two levels of work per year group in a mixed-age class. Clearly, specific provision must be made for particular children who have individual education plans.

This marks a change in attitude to teaching the class, and has repercussions for record-keeping and assessment plans. Given that we are now:

- teaching the same topic to all the children
- practising pre-requisite skills in the mental/oral starter with all the children
- dividing into no more than three groups for the main part of the lesson

it is no longer necessary to write notes on the progress of every single child. The majority of each year group will be engaged in the same tasks, and studying the same mathematics at the same level. For these children, it is important to record deviations from the norm: i.e. what happens if the child was not able to cope with the work given, or if they found it too easy.

It remains as true as ever that children are individuals, who do not all learn or develop at the same rate. The following points may help teachers to cope with the inevitable differences between children when they are teaching the whole class and 'keeping all the children together'.

It is important to remember that the class may be divided into more than three *groups* as long as there are no more than three *levels* of work. Most teachers organise their class so that the children are seated in small groups. They may, therefore, have two or three 'tables' working at the same level, probably on the same activity. One or two more, or less able children may be working on an activity more appropriate for their ability.

Once the topic has been introduced to the children, and the main direct teaching has taken place, it is usual to split the class into groups for most of them to work more independently, and to practise or apply what they have just been taught. It is only in this way that children come to make this knowledge their own. It is also the means of finding out who has, and who has not, grasped the mathematics, and therefore assessing the need for further teaching or practice. It is a sensible strategy to work with the children who need most help first, since this is the group who are likely to need some further teaching before they are able to work independently or semi-independently on the topic.

There is (as the Numeracy Strategy makes clear) a 'hierarchy' of types of work which can be used when planning for groups of children. It is easiest for children to do work which has been laid out for them, and where few decisions have to be made about what is to be done. Thus Workbooks, or Photocopy Masters, are relatively simple for children to use independently from the teacher. Textbooks, where the children are given help with laying out their work, and the tasks are still well-defined, are also useful in enabling independent work. Work written on the board is more difficult, since children must lay it out for themselves. Activities involving structural materials, coins, number cards, grids, etc., can require quite a high input from the teacher.

Abacus provides materials for the different levels of work suggested by the Numeracy Strategy and also helps to organise the class so that you are working in a focused way with one group, as recommended. The Activity Book indicates activities targeted at three ability levels, and the Workbooks and Textbooks allow for children who find the work moderately easy to engage, with extension activities. It is easiest to organise the class so that those children who are working relatively independently have suitably contained activities – (e.g. Workbooks, Photocopy Masters, Textbooks), whilst those children who have the benefit of your focused attention engage in the activities which enable further directed teaching.

Special needs

Children who have Individual Education Plans (IEPs) will normally be included in the whole class parts of the lesson, such as the mental/oral starter, the plenary, and the introduction to the topic in the main teaching activity. It will be rare for a child to be excluded from these parts of the lesson, although behaviour management, or their skills level, may mean that they are only present for some of these activities. Once a topic has been introduced, the teacher will need to ensure that the follow-up activities are at a level which is appropriate for the child and which fit with their development plan. Normally children with IEPs will work on the same topic as the remainder of the class, but at a lower level or by addressing some of the pre-requisite skills needed to engage with that topic. This work can be selected either from the Abacus Unit itself, drawing upon appropriate activities, or from related Units covered earlier.

7 Teaching strategies

Abacus is conceived around the conviction that active teaching is at the heart of an effective mathematics lesson. Although most teachers never analyse what they do, teaching in fact includes a number of different components. Good, lively and direct teaching involves:

- Demonstrating or modelling a strategy or skill. This can include showing children how to do something or providing an image to help them to understand a strategy.
- Instructing, or talking children through a procedure or process to be followed.
- Explaining and illustrating – providing reasons and giving examples.
- Questioning and discussing, so that teachers actively encourage children's engagement with mathematics.
- Practising, rehearsing and reinforcing a skill or a set of operations. Teachers use repetition to increase familiarity, and practice to help consolidation of strategies or procedures.
- Evaluating children's responses and dealing with errors.

In order to teach a good lesson, you need to have a clear sense of **what** they are teaching and **how** to teach it, using a set of strategies. This means knowing which images or resources can be used to demonstrate or model a particular mathematical concept or operation. The Abacus Teacher Cards outline the objectives clearly, so that you know precisely what is being covered in each Unit. It can be a good idea to share a key objective with the children, often writing it at the top of the flipchart or board. *Today, we are going to learn how to add ten or twenty or thirty to a number.*

The Teacher Card also describes the images or models which can be used to teach each topic effectively (the Abacus authors have brought a great deal of expertise and effort to bear in this area). Teachers can be confident of having a range of ways to represent or demonstrate the mathematics involved, to enable children to understand and apply what they are learning.

When teaching children from 4 to 7 years old, it is almost always possible to break down the representation of a piece of mathematics into two stages. First, children need a model – a way of understanding the appropriate mathematical concept. Second, they need to be shown how to perform the operation involved.

For example, when beginning to teach addition we want children to understand that addition is not only about combining two sets of objects, but also about counting on along a number line. So, 5 + 2 can be modelled by adding two bricks to a tower of five (making it more likely that children will count on from '5', rather than counting the bricks in the first tower). Addition will also be modelled using a number line or track, starting from 5 and counting on two more. The towers and the number line both provide a representation of the mathematics involved. They enable children to make sense of what they are being taught and to hold visual images in their heads.

However, children also need a practical and easy way of doing any appropriate additions. In this example, they will almost certainly be taught how to use fingers to count on when performing additions (relating back to the model, e.g. the number line). *Start at 5 and count on two more, using fingers. Six, seven. The answer is seven.* The demonstration or modelling uses the towers of bricks or the number line, but the method of doing the additions will use fingers.

Abacus draws upon a wide variety of models, images and strategies to demonstrate and explain the mathematical concepts and operations which children encounter in their first three years at school. These include:

- number lines 1 to 20, and beyond
- number grids (0 to 99 or 1 to 100)
- small digits cards
- towers and large bricks
- interlocking cubes in sets of ten, and loose cubes
- place-value cards
- money, particularly 10p coins and 1p coins to help with place-value
- a coat-hanger with key rings or pegs attached
- toys and role-play (shopping, giving change, etc.).

In addition, Abacus develops a number of effective and pragmatic strategies for children to use when performing mathematical operations, such as adding two numbers. These include:

- fingers – used to help count, count on or back, double numbers, learn number pairs for numbers up to and including ten, count in twos, fives and tens, and recognise odd and even numbers
- number lines or tracks – used to help count on, find a difference, count back, compare numbers, round to the nearest multiple of ten
- number grids (0 to 99 or 1 to 100) – used to help count to 100, add or subtract tens or multiples of ten, count in steps of various sizes, compare numbers or to find the next multiple of ten
- place-value cards – used to help compare numbers and understand the value of each digit.

Questioning

There are two types of question which are used in teaching mathematics – open questions and closed questions. Open questions are generally addressed to the whole class. Closed questions can be targeted at particular children (though they too can be addressed to a large group). You need to consider which type of question is most likely to achieve the response you require, as well as which will serve the mathematical end you have in mind. It is often true that a question asked in an 'open' form will achieve a much higher degree of interaction than the same question if asked in a closed format. For example, a closed question might be *What adds to 3 to make 10?* whereas a more open question would be *Who can tell me two numbers which add together to make 10?* The first question has only one answer, but the second can be used to generate a response from every pair of children in the room.

How do you expect the children to respond to your questions?

The traditional mode of teacher question and pupil answer, where children wave their hands in the air and one child is selected to answer, can result in frustrated children and only a few of the class taking part. Recent trials show that teachers are increasingly drawing on a range of resources in encouraging all the children in the class to respond to a question. The children can:

- use number cards, holding these up to show an answer
- all suggest answers, so that the teacher then records lots of different answers on the flipchart or board and then rehearses the operation with the class to see which answer is correct
- keep an answer hidden and then reveal it on a count of three
- all say or shout an answer in unison – particularly where an answer which you hope is on 'automatic pilot' is required, such as *Four and what make ten?*
- work in pairs to write down an answer, and then hand in papers (without names on).

We know, from the evidence of both research and practice over recent years, that questions and answers can provide a valuable means of creating an interactive teaching environment. One useful strategy is to give each child a 'maths partner' to work with in short bursts in question and answer sessions, or when playing whole class games. The first time the class work with their pairs may prove difficult, but they will soon start working well together and you will notice great improvements in their speaking and listening.

8 Specific guidance on mathematical content

In order to get the best out of the Abacus materials, you are advised to note the following points.

Counting

It is important that the sequence and naming structure of the number system becomes second nature to the children. Abacus encourages frequent practice at reciting numbers in sequence in a variety of different ways, with particular emphasis on counting in ones and in tens. The number line and a 1 to 100 number square are frequently used as models, and children are encouraged to use their fingers to enhance the development of their counting skills.

Place-value

At Key Stage 1, children need to develop a solid foundation in the understanding of the place-value aspect of our number system, progressing from tens and units to hundreds, tens and units. They need to understand that the '4' in 47, for example, stands for four tens, that 47 lies between the 'tens' forty and fifty, and that it is nearer to fifty. 'Place-value' cards are suggested as a model to aid this understanding, alongside Base Ten material.

In Year 2 children will begin to become familiar with 3-digit numbers. There is a marked tendency in modern day life to say these numbers as strings of digits, 'two, four, five' (like a telephone number) rather than 'two hundred and forty-five'. It is important that children perceive 3-digit numbers as numbers and not as strings of digits. Insisting that the children read them properly is one way of ensuring this.

Addition and subtraction

Abacus places strong emphasis on the development of children's mental addition and subtraction skills, and children are taught a variety of strategies to enhance this development. The emphasis placed on reciting numbers in sequence lays the foundation for using the strategies of counting on and counting back to add and subtract. The number line and the 1 to 100 number square are frequently used to model both addition and subtraction.

Many mental addition and subtraction skills depend on a sound knowledge of addition pairs (or bonds) to 10, to 20, to 100, for example. Abacus places a great emphasis on the recognition of addition pairs to 10 in Key Stage 1. This means more than knowing that, for example, 3 and 7 make 10 and includes the child being able to respond immediately with one member of the 'pair', when hearing the other.

Abacus encourages a carefully structured development in the use of appropriate vocabulary associated with addition and subtraction. The long term aim is for children to recognise all the different ways of reading the '+' and '–' signs, and the '=' sign. The vocabulary suggested on the Teacher Cards has a development with this aim in view.

Multiplication and division

Abacus introduces children to the concept of multiplication and to the use of the multiplication sign in Abacus 2. The ×2, ×5 and ×10 multiplication tables are introduced. It is strongly felt by the authors of Abacus, based on classroom experiences, that the recorded representation of 'six twos' is '6 × 2' (and not '2 × 6'). This is read in different ways as 'six twos', 'six lots of two', 'six groups of two', and so on.

Division is introduced in Year 2 both from the perspective of 'sharing' and of 'grouping'. As children progress through Abacus beyond Year 2, the emphasis is placed on the 'grouping' concept of sharing, which naturally leads to linking division to multiplication. Thus the development of division skills will be strongly linked to the development of multiplication skills.

Money

Abacus uses money to provide a 'real life' and familiar context within which to locate many numerical operations and concepts. Children are encouraged to see 'hundreds, tens and units' in terms of pound coins, ten pence pieces and one pence pieces. All children will regard money and coins as both interesting and important. Its use as a structured model for place-value capitalises on this interest.

Children see adults using, enjoying and worrying about money. They are well aware of the importance accorded to money in our society. They know that money transactions are an essential part of our daily lives. Unlike coloured bricks, blocks or interlocking cubes, money has an importance and a reality outside the primary classroom. It is this fact that makes money such a powerful teaching tool. Children want to operate using money. They want to understand how money works, and to participate in the adult transactions that they see around them.

Measures

In all aspects of measures (e.g. length, weight, capacity, angle), Abacus provides pupils with activities which develop the important skill of estimation. Providing children with estimating experiences enhances their understanding of the measurement concepts involved.

Weight and mass

Throughout this stage of work in Abacus the work 'weight' is used in preference to 'mass'. Scientifically, the weight is the force exerted by the earth's gravitational field on an object: weight can then be crudely interpreted as the pull towards the ground. The mass of an object is the quantity of matter it contains. The force of attraction varies with the position of the object, but the quantity of matter remains fixed. So, for example, an astronaut weighs less on the Moon because the Moon's gravitational attraction is weaker than the Earth's. The astronaut's mass – the amount of matter in his body – is unchanged.

The weight of an object can be found by using a spring balance, bathroom scale or direct-reading kitchen scale, but the mass has to be found by using balance scales where an object is placed in one pan and a balance obtained by placing objects of known mass in the other.

Though this distinction between weight and mass is clear to the scientist, it is rarely made in daily life. Later in Abacus, when units have been developed and understood, this distinction will be relatively easy to grasp, but at this stage the word weight is used in accordance with its everyday usage. If you are concerned about this decision, the word mass may be used when it is obviously more appropriate, but the intention is that no undue worry should be centred around the distinction between the two words.

Shapes

Although the correct mathematical name for the 'corner' of a 2-d and 3-d shape is vertex (plural 'vertices'), Abacus uses the more easily recognised word 'corner' in Abacus 2, and introduces the word 'vertex' in Abacus 3. The correct terminology is 'sides' and 'vertices' for 2-d shapes, and 'faces', 'edges' and 'vertices' for 3-d shapes.

9. Framework for teaching mathematics matching chart

2

Numbers and the number system

Counting, properties of numbers and number sequences

Say the number names in order to at least 100, from and back to zero.	N1, N34
Count reliably up to 100 objects by grouping them: for example, in tens, then in fives or twos.	N1
Describe and extend simple number sequences:	
count on or back in ones or tens, starting from any two-digit number	N13, N15, N25, N28
count in hundreds from and back to zero	Warm-ups, N34, M2
count on in twos from and back to zero or any small number, **and recognise odd and even numbers** to at least 30	N7, N12, N28
count on in steps of 3, 4 or 5 to at least 30, from and back to zero, then from and back to any given small number.	N20, N25, N28
Begin to recognise two-digit multiples of 2, 5 or 10.	N12, N13, N25

Place-value and ordering

Read and write whole numbers to at least 100 in figures and words.	N2
Know what each digit in a two-digit number represents, including 0 as a place holder, and partition two-digit numbers into a multiple of ten and ones (TU).	N2, N16
Use and begin to read the vocabulary of comparing and ordering numbers, including ordinal numbers to 100.	N9, N22, N29, N36
Use the = sign to represent equality.	N37
Compare two given two-digit numbers, say which is more or less, and give a number which lies between them.	N9
Say the number that is 1 or 10 more or less than any given two-digit number.	N22, N34
Order whole numbers to at least 100, and position them on a number line and 100 square.	N2, N29, N34

Estimating

Use and begin to read the vocabulary of estimation and approximation; give a sensible estimate of at least 50 objects.	N2, N28
Round numbers less than 100 to the nearest 10.	N36

Fractions

Begin to recognise and find one half and one quarter of shapes and small numbers of objects.	N14, N27, N41
Begin to recognise that two halves or four quarters make one whole and that two quarters and one half are equivalent.	N27, N41

* Key objectives are highlighted in **bold type**.

Framework for teaching mathematics matching chart (cont.)

Calculations

Understanding addition and subtraction

Extend understanding of the operations of addition and subtraction.	N3, N5, N6, N10, N17, N18, N19
Use and begin to read the related vocabulary.	Warm-ups
Use the +, – and = signs to record mental additions and subtractions in a number sentence, and recognise the use of a symbol such as □ or Δ to stand for an unknown number. Recognise that addition can be done in any order, but not subtraction: for example, 3 + 21 = 21 + 3, but 21 – 3 ≠ 3 – 21.	N21, N31, N37
Understand that more than two numbers can be added. Begin to add three single-digit numbers mentally (totals up to about 20) of three two-digit numbers with the help of apparatus (totals up to 100).	N30
Understand that subtraction is the inverse of addition (subtraction reverses addition).	N37

Rapid recall of addition and subtraction facts

Know by heart:	
all addition and subtraction facts for each number to at least 10	N3
all pairs of numbers with a total of 20 (e.g. 13 + 7, 6 + 14)	N18, N31
all pairs of multiples of 10 with a total of 100 (e.g. 30 + 70).	N31

Mental calculation strategies (+ and –)

Use knowledge that addition can be done in any order to do mental calculations more efficiently. For example:	
put the larger number first and count on in tens or ones	N10
add three small numbers by putting the largest number first and / or finding a pair totalling 10	N30
partition into '5 and a bit' when adding 6, 7, 8 or 9, then recombine (e.g. 16 + 8 = 15 + 1 + 5 + 3 = 20 + 4 = 24)	N21
partition additions into tens and units, then recombine.	N21, N23
Find a small difference by counting up from the smaller to the larger number (e.g. 42 – 39).	N33
Identify near doubles, using doubles already known (e.g. 8 + 9, 40 + 41).	N17
Add/subtract 9 or 11: add/subtract 10 and adjust by 1.	N6, N19
Begin to add/subtract 19 or 21.	N6, N19
Use patterns of similar calculations.	Throughout
State the subtraction corresponding to a given addition, and vice versa.	N37
Use known number facts and place-value to add/subtract mentally.	N21, N23
Bridge through 10 to 20, then adjust.	N24

* Key objectives are highlighted in **bold type**.

Framework for teaching mathematics matching chart (cont.)

2

Understanding multiplication and division

Understand the operation of multiplication as repeated addition or as describing an array, and begin to understand division as grouping (repeated subtraction) or sharing.	N26, N39, N40
Use and begin to read the related vocabulary.	N12, N13, N25, N26, N39, N40
Use the ×, ÷ and = signs to record mental calculations in a number sentence, and recognise the use of a symbol such as □ or Δ to stand for an unknown number.	N12, N26, N39, N40
Know and use halving as the inverse of doubling.	N35

Rapid recall of multiplication and division facts

Know by heart:	
multiplication facts for the 2 and 10 times-tables	N12, N13, N25
doubles of all number to 10 and the corresponding halves	N17, N32, N35, N38
multiplication facts up to 5 × 5 (e.g. 4 × 3).	N39
Begin to know multiplication facts for the 5 times-table.	N25
Derive quickly:	
division facts corresponding to the 2 and 10 times-tables	N40
doubles of all numbers to at least 15 (e.g. 11 + 11 or 11 × 2)	N32, N38
doubles of multiples of 5 to 50 (e.g. 20 × 2 or 35 × 2)	N32, N38
halves of multiples of 10 to 100 (e.g. half of 70).	N41

Mental calculation strategies (× and ÷)

Use known number facts and place-value to carry out mentally simple multiplications and divisions.	Warm-ups

Checking results of calculations

Repeat addition in a different order.	Warm-ups
Check with an equivalent calculation.	Warm-ups

Solving problems

Making decisions

Choose and use appropriate operations and efficient calculation strategies (e.g. mental, mental with jottings) to solve problems.	N5, N11, N18, N21

Reasoning about numbers or shapes

Solve mathematical problems or puzzles, recognise simple patterns and relationships, generalise and predict. Suggest extensions by asking *What if ...?* or *What could I try next?*	N8, N38
Investigate a general statement about familiar numbers or shapes by finding examples that satisfy it.	Warm-ups, S1, S4
Explain how a problem was solved orally and, where appropriate, in writing.	N37

* Key objectives are highlighted in **bold type**.

Framework for Teaching Mathematics matching chart (cont.)

2

Problems involving 'real life', money or measures

Use mental addition and subtraction, simple multiplication and division, to solve simple word problems involving numbers in 'real life', money or measures, using one or two steps.	N5, N11, N18, N21, N38
Explain how the problem was solved.	N21, N23, N33, N37
Recognise all coins and begin to use £.p notation for money (for example, know that £4.65 indicates £4 and 65p).	N4
Find totals, give change, and work out which coins to pay.	N4, N11, N31, N37

Organising and using data

Solve a given problem by sorting, classifying and organising information in simple ways, such as: in a list or simple table, in a pictogram, in a block graph. Discuss and explain results.	D1, D2, D3, D4, D5

Measures, shape and space

Measures

Use and begin to read the vocabulary related to length, mass and capacity.	M1, M2, M5, M6, M8
Estimate, measure and compare lengths, masses and capacities, using standard units (m, cm, kg, litre).	M1, M2, M5, M6
Suggest suitable units and equipment for such measurements.	M2
Read a simple scale to the nearest labelled division, including using a ruler to draw and measure lines that to the nearest centimetre, recording estimates and measurements as '3 and a bit metres long' or about 8 centimetres' or 'nearly 3 kilograms heavy'.	M1, M2, M5, M8
Use and begin to read vocabulary related to time.	M3, M4, M7
Use units of time and know the relationships between them (second, minute, hour, day, week).	M10, M11
Suggest suitable units to estimate or measure time.	M7, M9, M10, M11
Order the months of the year.	M9
Read the time to the hour, half hour or quarter hour on an analogue clock and a 12-hour digital clock, and understand the notation 7:30.	M3, M4, M7

Shape and space

Use the mathematical names for common 3-D and 2-D shapes, including the pyramid, cylinder, pentagon, hexagon, octagon ...	S1, S3, S4
Sort shapes and describe some of their features, such as the number of sides and comers, symmetry (2-D shapes), or the shapes of faces and number of faces, edges and corners (3-D shapes).	S1, S4
Make and describe shapes, pictures and patterns using, for example, solid shapes, templates, pinboard and elastic bands, squared paper, a programmable robot ...	S3, S4
Relate solid shapes to pictures of them.	S1
Begin to recognise line symmetry.	S6
Use mathematical vocabulary to describe position, direction and movement: for example, describe, place, tick, draw or visualise objects in given positions.	S2
Recognise whole, half and quarter turns, to the left or right, clockwise or anticlockwise.	S2
Know that a right angle is a measure of a quarter turn, and recognise right angles in squares and rectangles.	S5
Give instructions for moving along a route in straight lines and round right-angled corners: for example, to pass through a simple maze ...	S2, S5

* Key objectives are highlighted in **bold type**.

10 Classroom materials

Materials provided in the *Resource Bank*

Number line (0 to 20) – large, double-sided, full-colour number cards, for demonstration
Number line (0 to 100) – medium, double-sided two-colour number cards, for demonstration
Class pack of small number cards (0 to 10) – 30 sets, for individual children
Group pack of small number cards (0 to 10) – 10 sets for group work
Group pack of small number cards (0 to 30) – 5 sets for group work
Pack of small number cards (0 to 100) – 1 set for group work
Wall chart pack (0 to 99 grid and 1 to 100 grid) – 6 sets for a school
Place-value cards (standard pack) – 5 sets of units, tens and hundreds
Place-value cards (extended pack) – 5 sets of units, tens, hundreds, thousands, tenths and hundredths.

Other specialised resources, such as small number grids and number tracks, are included as Photocopy Masters in the Activity Book.

Infant Games pack

24 games referenced to specific Teacher Card units.

Assumed mathematical materials in the classroom

Interlocking cubes
Counters
Spotty dice (1 to 6)
Numbered dice (1 to 6) and (0 to 5) and (1 to 10)
Calculators
Dominoes
Playing cards
Coins (real and plastic)
Base Ten equipment
Sets of plastic 2-d shapes
Sets of solid 3-d shapes
Containers (for Capacity)
Analogue clock with moveable hands
Digital clock
Sand timers or rocking timers
Seconds timer or stopclock
Weighing balances/weighing scales
Set of weights
Rulers/metre sticks/tape measures
Centicubes
Pegboards and pegs

Other materials

Washing line with pegs attached
Hoops
Cloth (Feely) bags
Blu-tack
Soft toys
Construction equipment
Coat-hanger and keyrings

11 Assessment grid (Key Stage 1)

To assist with statutory assessment, selected items from the level descriptions are included within the scheme. For each item, key stages within the scheme are identified. This gives you a quick reference for reporting progress. Each item is presented in the form:

I can...

read, write, count and order numbers up to 10. Abacus R N5, N8, N14

You can then quickly assess achievement using an on/off principle. The child **can do** or **cannot do**. There are no interim stages on the records.

- The system allows a cumulative record to develop.
- Each box can be completed in a variety of ways:
  - a simple tick or colouring in by you or pupil;
  - a colouring in using a different colour for each year: red for Reception, blue for Year 1, green for Year 2, ... yellow for Year 6;
  - or preferably a short comment on a particular child's attainment.

At the bottom of each box is a code showing where to check this particular statement (of the form Abacus R N5 – Abacus Reception Unit N5, or Abacus 1 N8 – Abacus 1 Unit N8 etc.). In some instances this will be at different stages within the scheme to match the development of individual children. Your observations during mental warm-ups, focused group work, or written evidence from Workbooks and Assessment sheets will provide plenty of evidence of achievement for each statement. The record sheets can also be used as: a prompt at the planning stage, part of a record of achievement, a tool for feeding back to parents, a check of a child's individual progress, an assessment of group or whole class progress.

The items included within the assessment grid are taken from the appropriate level descriptions of each attainment target in the National Curriculum. You will be able to use the cumulative information contained within the grid, together with your global view of the child's progress and any other factors you think appropriate, in coming to a decision about whether the child has successfully achieved the appropriate level within each attainment target.

There is no suggestion that the grid alone will provide the only evidence for making end of year or end of key stage assessments. Abacus is in full accord with the objectives in the National Curriculum in wanting these decisions to be based on the level description as a whole rather than simply a collection of disparate items.

Assessment grid: Key Stage 1
Number

2

Name________________________

I can …

Level 1	Level 2	Level 3
read, write, count and order numbers up to 10. Abacus R N5, N8, N14	read, write, count and order numbers up to 100. Abacus 1 N15	read, write, count and order numbers up to 1000. Abacus 2 N34
add and subtract with totals up to 10. Abacus R N19, N22	understand place-value in numbers to 100. Abacus 1 N9, N16 Abacus 2 N2, N16	understand and use place-value in numbers to 1000. Abacus 2 N36
know one more or less than a number (up to 10). Abacus R N3, N6	use mental recall of addition and subtraction facts to 10. Abacus 1 N11, N14, N18 Abacus 2 N3	use mental recall of addition and subtraction facts to 20. Abacus 2 N18, N31
recognise and make repeating patterns. Abacus 1 N22	know one or ten more/less than a number (up to 30). Abacus 1 N12, N28, N29	mentally recall the ×2, ×5 and ×10 multiplication tables and others up to 5 × 5. Abacus 2 N12, N13, N25, N39
	recognise sequences of numbers, including odd and even. Abacus 1 N8, N21, N34 Abacus 2 N7	use mental strategies to add and subtract numbers with two digits. Abacus 2 N6, N33 *Abacus 3*

Assessment grid: Key Stage 1
Shape, Space and Measures

2

Name________________________

I can ...

Level 1	Level 2	Level 3
use everyday language to describe properties of 2-d and 3-d shapes. Abacus R S1, S2	use mathematical language to describe 2-d and 3-d shapes and their properties. Abacus 1 S1, S3	classify 2-d and 3-d shapes using mathematical properties. Abacus 1 S4, S5 Abacus 2 S1, S4
measure and order objects by direct comparison. Abacus R M1, M2, M4, M5	use mathematical language to describe position, direction and movement. Abacus 1 S2, S6	recognise and use reflective symmetry. Abacus 1 S7 Abacus 2 S6
order events. Abacus R M6, M9	use standard and non-standard units to measure length and mass. Abacus 1 M2, M6	use non-standard and standard metric units of length, capacity, weight and time. Abacus 1 M2, M6 Abacus 2 M2, M5, M6, M10, M11

12 Getting started with Abacus

Making a number line

The image of a line of numbers is a very powerful assistance to children in helping them to perform number operations and develop an understanding of how the number system works. Abacus makes use of number cards pegged onto a washing line. The easiest way to make this line – which can remain hanging up in the classroom throughout the year – is as follows:

(i) You will need a length of thickish string, some pegs and some matchsticks.
(ii) Thread the required number of pegs (ten to start with and then twenty later in the year) onto the string. Do not clip the pegs on in the usual way. Thread the string through the small horizontal round hole in the middle of the metal spring in the peg. The pegs will then remain attached to the string while cards are clipped in and out of them.
(iii) Put a small piece of matchstick in through each hole to wedge the string firm. This stops the pegs sliding along the string. They can still be opened and shut to hold cards in the usual way.
(iv) Clip on the number cards (provided in the Resource Bank).

This number line makes an immensely powerful resource in the classroom. It is useful to have a permanent number line up around the walls of the classroom with numbers up to 30, and then as the year progresses, with the numbers up to 100 added. This means that the children can look at this 'visual aid' to help them with their work. It also provides the powerful image of the sequence of numbers which we wish them to internalise.

Have a smaller number line on hand to use for all the activities and lessons where it is mentioned in Abacus. This number line should also be permanently displayed and can be used for a quick 'early' mathematics activity each day. Swap two numbers around. Can the children say which two have been swapped? Remove one number. Which one is missing? Turn one number back to front, e.g. 15 becomes 51. Can the children say which number in the sequence is no longer correct?

Introducing Abacus

Abacus may be introduced to a whole school at once, or it may be started with a class of pupils who have come from other schools, and who have not previously been working with the Abacus approach. In order to help those teachers who are introducing Abacus to children for the first time, these key skills are an assumed foundation for the children entering Year 2.

12. Getting started with Abacus

Year 2 Key Skills

- To count in ones from any small number
- To count in multiples of ten
- To begin to count in tens from a small number
- To add by counting on, e.g. 5 + 4
- To know addition pairs to 10
- To subtract by counting back, e.g. 9 – 3
- To recognise and name common 2-d shapes: square, rectangle, circle, triangle
- To recognise and name common 3-d shapes: cube, cuboid, pyramid, cone, sphere.

13 Planning

The heart of good teaching is understanding the relationship between **what** is taught and **how** best to teach it. The plan is your way of making this connection explicit. In order to be an effective (even excellent) teacher, it is not necessary to spend hours planning. Indeed, sometimes overplanning can be counter-productive. It is necessary to have:

- **Long term plans**, which enable each teacher to know that the pre-requisite skills and strategies needed for a particular piece of mathematics have been covered in previous years.
- **Medium term plans**, which enable each teacher to pace the content coverage over the course of the year, and also to give the appropriate weightings to each part of the curriculum.
- **Short term plans,** which enable each teacher to know exactly what they are teaching, and how they are teaching it, at the start of the topic.

The National Numeracy Strategy states that it is not necessary for teachers to draw up daily lesson plans, providing that the weekly plan has sufficient structure, content and classroom management information.

Long term planning

Any long term plan is now effectively supplied by the Framework for Teaching Mathematics. This outlines the key objectives (and all the other teaching objectives) for each year of the primary curriculum. In very particular circumstances, such as those pertaining to some Special Schools, it may be necessary to adapt the Framework, but for most schools, it supplies an essential long term plan, which staff can use and become familiar with.

Medium term planning

The medium term plan can also be derived from the Framework for Teaching Mathematics. You can copy the Medium term planning grids from the Framework and use them to construct your own individual medium term plans. Exemplar planning grids, mapping the Abacus Teacher Cards and objectives on to the Framework structure are provided at the end of the book, from page 42.

Because of the flexibility of the Abacus Teacher Cards, it is quite easy for you to alter this order, and to adapt it to suit the needs of your own class. The lesson objectives are clearly stated on each Teacher Card and it is, therefore, simple to postpone a Unit, or to exchange one Unit with another, if so desired.

Using Abacus, the time spent on long term and medium term planning has been cut to an absolute minimum. The exemplar planning grids we provide will ensure that the teaching objectives in the Framework for Teaching Mathematics are covered, and that the order and balance of the topics is preserved.

Short term planning

Given the long and medium term planning, the short term planning becomes a relatively simple task. Each week, you select the appropriate Abacus resources for the Unit(s) to be covered, study the Teacher Card(s) noting the teaching objectives and the resources needed, decide how to balance Units (Teacher Cards) over the week and notes the objectives for each day on your weekly plan. You should record the resources to be used, and the ways in which you plan to teach the topics concerned. This information is all clearly outlined on the Teacher Cards.

The format of the weekly plan may vary from school to school, although each school will need to have discussed this and to have agreed a common model. Many schools will choose to use the sample plan outline provided by the Numeracy Strategy training materials. Weekly plans can be brief, but will certainly be more detailed for Monday and Tuesday than for later in the week. Any weekly plan will need to incorporate the following information:

- Clear objectives for the mental/oral section. *[Appropriate Warm-up activity]*
- Clear objectives for the main teaching activity. *[Teacher Card, front]*
- Brief outline of the mental/oral activity. *[Appropriate Warm-up activity]*
- Brief outline of the main teaching activity specifying:
  - the model or image being used to teach this topic
  - the resources needed for the lesson
  - the organisation of the class (whole class, groups, paired work...). *[All on Teacher Card]*
- Indication of the teacher's focus (group, individuals ...).
- Outline of any differentiated activities. *[Teacher Card, back]*
- Key vocabulary, including key questions. *[Teacher Card]*
- Learning outcomes. *[Teacher Card, back]*
- Brief outline of possible points for the plenary. *[Teacher Card, back]*

It is therefore no exaggeration to say that all of this information can be obtained from the Abacus materials, in particular the Teacher Card and related resources for each Unit. Teachers will need to study the Abacus resources which accompany each Unit and plan their week's lessons accordingly. The questions of classroom management which need to be noted on the plan can be decided in relation to the activities you select from the Activity Book (or the Games Pack) and also from the Workbook or Textbook pages, Photocopy Masters, the Simmering Activities, Mental Warm-up Activities and Homework Book.

Once a detailed weekly plan has been drawn up, teachers will not need a lesson plan for each day. It is certainly true that, as the teaching progresses, the weekly plan will need to be modified and more detail added for the end of the week. However, this does not necessitate starting afresh, but rather adapting what has already been outlined.

Summary

The starting point for the weekly plan is the medium-term plan, which is drawn from the Framework (exemplars for Abacus are provided at the end of this book). The weekly plan needs to provide clear information about:

- what you are teaching – clear objectives for each part of the lesson each day
- how you are teaching it – outline of the teaching in each part
- how the class is to be managed – any differentiated activities and your focus each day
- what the children have learned and how you will evaluate this.

Once you have a good weekly plan, daily lesson plans are unnecessary.

Within Abacus, all the necessary information to enable you to plan as above is available in a simple and unambiguous form on the Teacher Card for each Unit.

Planning grids

The tables on the following pages show one way of matching the Abacus Units to the Numeracy Framework Planning Grids. They are arranged termly.

You may wish to match the Abacus Units to the Planning Grids in a different order, or you may wish to use your own planning grids. Clearly, whichever order you use, your ongoing evaluation and assessment will inform the development of the scheme of work during the course of the year.

Exemplar planning grid: autumn

Note: In the grid, the Abacus Unit refers to the main teaching focus of the lesson. Mental and oral skills, such as counting, will be practised every day, using the Mental Warm-up Activities.

Unit	Topic	Abacus Unit	Teaching points	Notes
1	Counting, properties of numbers and number sequences	N1 Numbers to 100	To recite number names from 1 to 100 and back To count a set of objects from 1 to 100	
2-4	Place-value, ordering, estimating, rounding	N2 Place-value	To read and write numbers to at least 100 To recognise the relationship between tens and units To estimate a number of objects up to 50 To order 2-digit numbers	
	Understanding + and – Mental calculation strategies (+ and –)	N3 Addition	To rehearse recognition of addition pairs to 10 To recognise amounts of money which total 10p	
	Money and 'real life' problems Making decisions and checking results	N4 Money	To recognise the relationship between coins (1p to £2) To exchange a coin for its equivalent amount in smaller coins To find total values of coins	
		N5 Subtraction	To understand subtraction as taking away To subtract from a number by counting back (not crossing ten) To solve subtraction problems in real life	
		N6 Addition	To add 10, 20 or 30 to a 2-digit number To add 11 or 12 to a number by adding 10 and adjusting To add 10p or 20p to an amount of money	
5-6	Measures, including problems	M1 Length	To rehearse measuring lengths using a non-standard measure To measure length in centimetres	
		M2 Length	To measure length in metres To recognise and use the relationship between metres and centimetres	
	Shape and space Reasoning about shapes	S1 3-d shape	To rehearse recognition and naming of 3-d shapes: cube, cuboid, pyramid, sphere To recognise and name cylinders and cones To sort 3-d shapes based on type of face	
		S2 Angle	To recognise clockwise and anticlockwise turns To follow instructions related to position	
7	Assess and review			

Unit	Topic	Abacus Unit	Teaching points	Notes
8	Counting, properties of numbers and number sequences	N7 Numbers to 100	To count on and back in ones and twos (from 0 to 100) To recognise odd and even numbers	
	Reasoning about numbers	N8 Number patterns	To investigate patterns with dice and number cards To reason about numbers, generating simple patterns and making predictions	
9-11	Place-value, ordering, estimating, rounding Understanding + and –	N9 Ordering	To compare two 2-digit numbers, recognising the larger and smaller To recognise numbers which lie between two 2-digit numbers	
	Mental calculation strategies (+ and –) Money and 'real life' problems	N10 Addition	To rehearse adding by counting on, when adding two 1-digit numbers crossing ten To recognise that numbers can be added in any order, and the largest number can be put first	
	Making decisions and checking results	N11 Money	To reinforce the concepts relating to money (i.e. buying and selling) To select the fewest coins to pay for amounts (up to 50p)	
10-11	Understanding × and ÷ Mental calculation strategies (× and ÷)	N12 Multiplication	To count in twos To introduce '×' notation To begin to recognise how many there are in different sets of twos	
	Money and 'real life' problems Making decisions and checking results	N13 Multiplication	To count in tens To rehearse the use of '×' notation To learn multiplication facts (× 10)	
	Fractions	N14 Fractions	To recognise halves of shapes To recognise quarters of shapes	
12-13	Measures, and time, including problems	M3 Time	To read the time to the hour and half hour on analogue clocks To read the time to the hour and half hour on digital clocks To use the vocabulary related to time	
		M4 Time	To rehearse reading the time to the hour and half hour on analogue clocks To read the time to the quarter hour on analogue clocks To use the vocabulary related to time	
	Handling data	D1 Sorting	To sort objects based on two non-distinct criteria using a Venn diagram	
		D2 Sorting	To sort objects based on two non-distinct criteria using a Carroll diagram	
14	Assess and review			

Exemplar planning grid: spring

Note: In the grid, the Abacus Unit refers to the main teaching focus of the lesson. Mental and oral skills, such as counting, will be practised every day, using the Mental Warm-up Activities.

Unit	Topic	Abacus Unit	Teaching points	Notes
1	Counting, properties of numbers and number sequences	N15 Numbers to 100	To count on and back in tens from any 2-digit number	
2-4	Place-value, ordering, estimating, rounding	N16 Place-value	To recognise the place-value of digits in a 2-digit number To partition a number into tens and units	
	Understanding + and – Mental calculation strategies (+ and –)	N17 Addition	To recognise doubles of numbers up to 10 by adding To add by using known doubles	
	Money and 'real life' problems	N18 Addition	To recognise addition pairs (up to 10) To solve 'real life' problems involving addition To recognise '0' as a set with no objects	
	Making decisions and checking results	N19 Subtraction	To subtract 10 and multiples of 10 from a 2-digit number To subtract 11 and 12 from a 2-digit number To subtract 10p and 20p from amounts (up to £1)	
5-6	Measures, including problems	M5 Weight	To rehearse measuring weight using a non-standard unit To recognise the need for a standard unit of measure for weight To measure weight using kilograms and grams	
		M6 Capacity	To rehearse measuring capacity using a non-standard unit To recognise the need for a standard unit of capacity To measure capacity using litres To compare the capacities of different containers	
	Shape and space Reasoning about shapes	S3 2-d shape	To rehearse recognition and naming of 2-d shapes To begin to name pentagons, hexagons, octagons, heptagons	
		S4 2-d shape	To rehearse recognition and naming of 2-d shapes To sort 2-d shapes based on numbers of sides and corners	
7	Assess and review			

Unit	Topic	Abacus Unit	Teaching points	Notes
8	Counting, properties of numbers and number sequences	N20 Numbers to 100	To count in steps of 3, 4 or 5 to at least 30, and back	
	Reasoning about numbers	N21 Addition/ subtraction	To recognise when to add and when to subtract in the context of money problems To add or subtract 1-digit numbers to or from teen numbers To partition numbers using knowledge of addition pairs	
9	Place-value, ordering, estimating, rounding	N22 Place-value	To say the number that is one more or less than a 2-digit number To say the number that is ten more or less than a 2-digit number	
	Understanding + and – Mental calculation strategies (+ and –)	N23 Addition	To add a 1-digit number to a 'teen' number To partition numbers using knowledge of addition pairs To use coins to find totals, crossing 10p and 20p	
	Money and 'real life' problems Making decisions	N24 Subtraction	To subtract a 1-digit number from a 'teen' number To partition numbers using knowledge of addition/subtraction facts To subtract a 1-digit number from a 'twenties' number	
10	Understanding × and ÷ Mental calculation strategies (× and ÷)	N25 Multiplication	To count in tens and fives To rehearse the use of '×' notation To rehearse multiplication facts (×10) To learn multiplication facts (×5)	
	Money and 'real life' problems	N26 Division	To divide by sharing equally a set of objects To begin to use the '÷' sign To begin to understand the concept of remainder	
	Making decisions and checking results Fractions	N27 Fractions	To recognise one half, one quarter and one third of shapes To begin to recognise that two halves, three thirds and four quarters make a whole To introduce fraction notation, i.e. $\frac{1}{2}$, $\frac{1}{3}$, $\frac{1}{4}$	
11-12	Measures, and time, including problems	M7 Time	To rehearse the time to the quarter hour on analogue clocks To read the time to the quarter hour on digital clocks To use the vocabulary related to time	
	Handling data	D3 Block graphs	To construct and interpret a block graph	
		D4 Sorting	To sort numbers based on two non-distinct criteria using a Venn diagram To order numbers using 'more than' and 'less than'	
13	Assess and review			

Exemplar planning grid: summer

Note: In the grid, the Abacus Unit refers to the main teaching focus of the lesson. Mental and oral skills, such as counting, will be practised every day, using the Mental Warm-up Activities.

Unit	Topic	Abacus Unit	Teaching points	Notes
1	Counting, properties of numbers and number sequences	N28 Numbers to 100	To count large numbers of objects, grouping in tens and fives To estimate and choose the more likely estimate To recognise odd and even numbers (up to 100)	
2-4	Place-value, ordering, estimating, rounding	N29 Ordering	To order a set of 1-digit and 2-digit numbers from smallest to largest	
	Understanding + and – Mental calculation strategies (+ and –)	N30 Addition	To add three 1-digit numbers To look for tens or put the larger number first	
		N31 Addition/ subtraction	To recognise addition pairs to 20 and totals which make 20p To find change for 20p To recognise addition pairs of multiples of 10, to make 100	
	Money and 'real life' problems	N32 Addition	To double all numbers to 15 (using money) To double multiples of five to 50	
	Making decisions and checking results	N33 Addition/ subtraction	To find the difference between two numbers (by counting on) To find small differences between two 2-digit numbers	
5-6	Measures, including problems	M8 Capacity	To measure capacity using standard and non-standard units To recognise the need for calibration	
		M9 Time	To recognise and order the months of the year To relate particular months to seasons of the year	
	Shape and space Reasoning about shapes	S5 Angle	To recognise a right angle To make a right-angle measure	
		S6 Symmetry	To recognise lines of symmetry To create symmetrical shapes by folding and cutting paper	
7	Assess and review			

Unit	Topic	Abacus Unit	Teaching points	Notes
8	Counting, properties of numbers and number sequences	N34 Numbers to 1000	To recite numbers in order beyond 100 To recognise 'one more' or 'one less' than a 3-digit number To order a set of 3-digit numbers To count on in hundreds from 0 to 900 and back	
	Reasoning about numbers	N35 Doubling/ halving	To recognise the concept of doubling, using addition of two equal amounts (up to 20) To introduce halving as the inverse of doubling (up to half of 20)	
9	Place-value, ordering, estimating, rounding	N36 Place-value	To round a 2-digit number to its nearest ten	
	Understanding + and – Mental calculation strategies (+ and –)	N37 Addition/ subtraction	To recognise links between addition and subtraction To find totals and change (using real coins) To begin to recognise number facts	
	Money and 'real life' problems Making decisions	N38 Addition	To rehearse doubling numbers to 15, and multiples of 5 (to 50) To solve real life problems using doubles facts	
10-11	Understanding × and ÷ Mental calculation strategies (× and ÷)	N39 Multiplication	To consolidate the concept of multiplication To recognise the commutativity of multiplication ($3 \times 5 = 5 \times 3$) using arrays To use the '×' sign	
	Money and 'real life' problems Making decisions and checking results	N40 Division	To introduce division as 'grouping' To begin to recognise the relationship between division and multiplication using arrays To use the '÷' sign To understand the concept of 'remainder'	
	Fractions	N41 Fractions	To find one half, one quarter or one third of a quantity or a number of objects To recognise that two quarters are the same as one half To use fraction notation	
12-13	Measures, and time, including problems	M10 Time	To recognise relationships between short units of time: seconds, minutes, hours	
		M11 Time	To recognise relationships between long units of time: hours, days, weeks	
	Handling data	D5 Tables	To sort data by listing it in a table To interpret simple tables	
14	Assess and review			